#HR LIFE

HUMAN RESOURCES

COLORING BOOK FOR HR PROFESSIONALS

30 FUNNY, SNARKY AND SARCASTIC QUOTES FOR INSPIRATION AND MOTIVATION

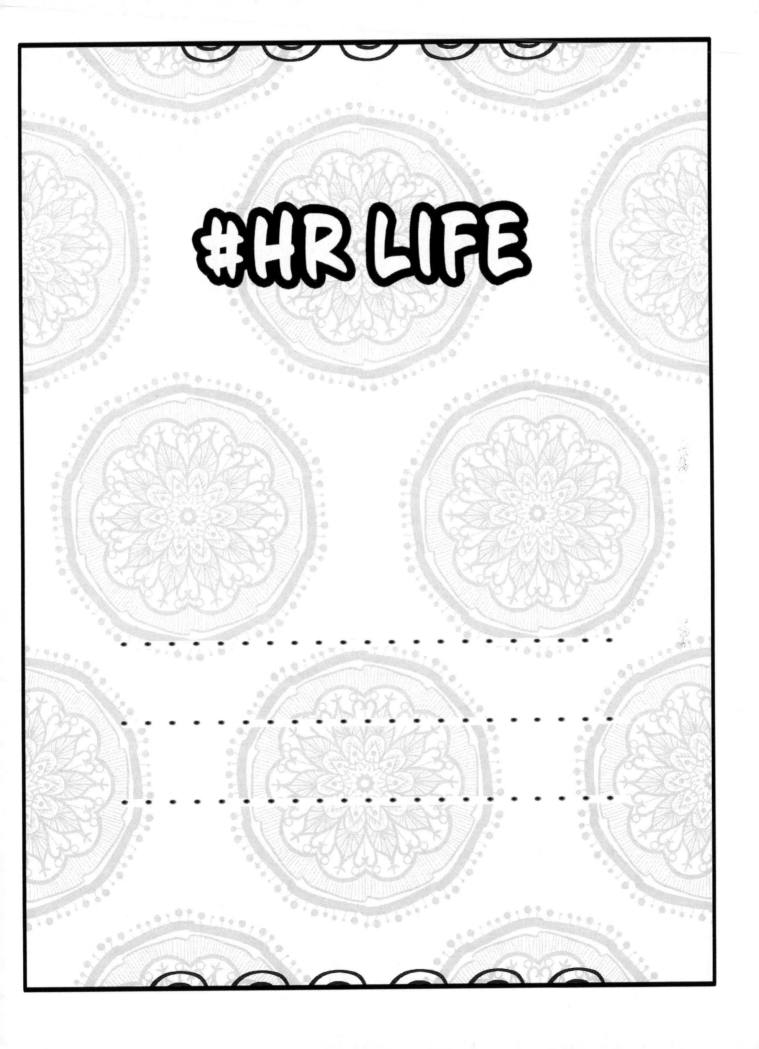

#HR LIFE

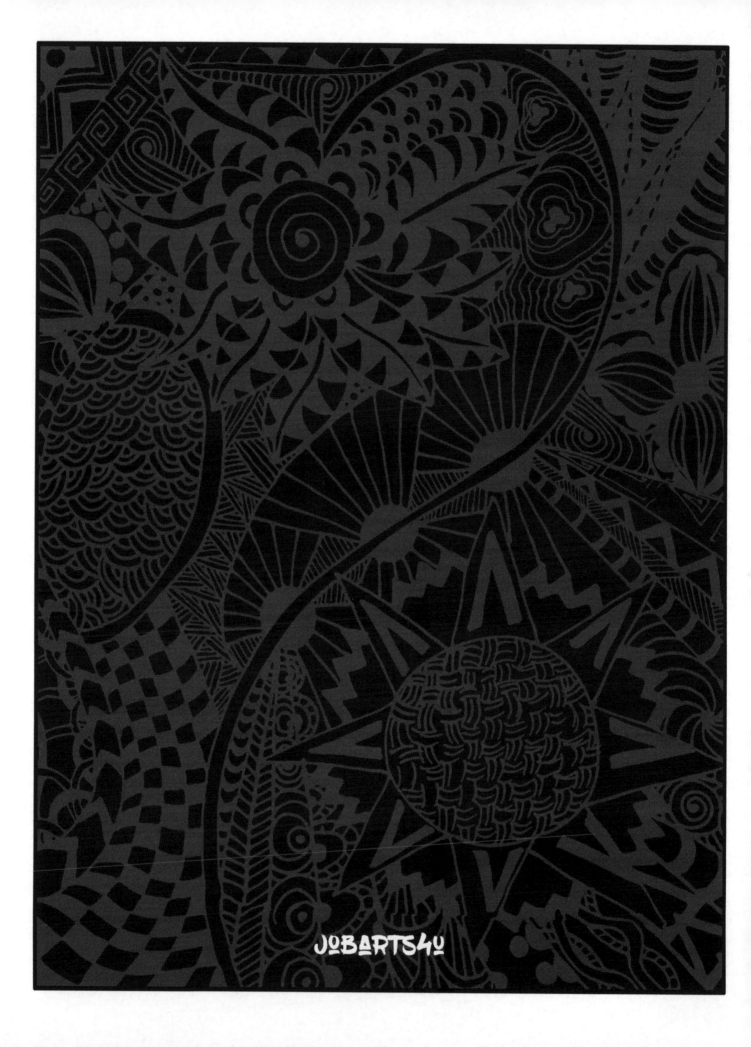

TEST THE COLORS HERE

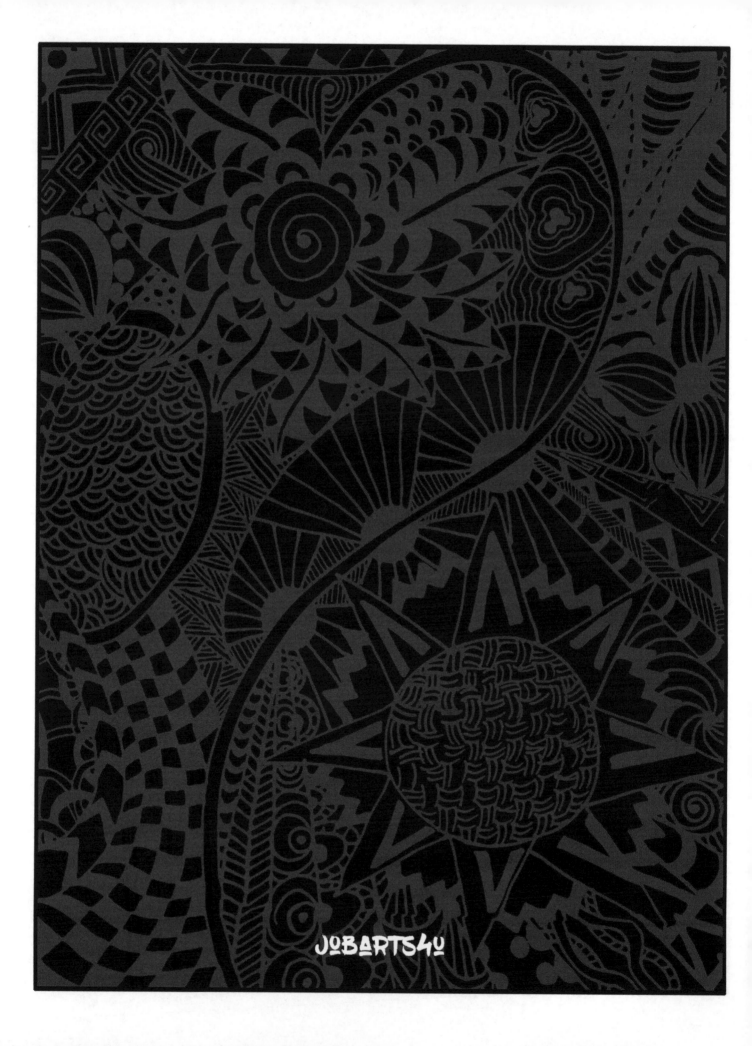

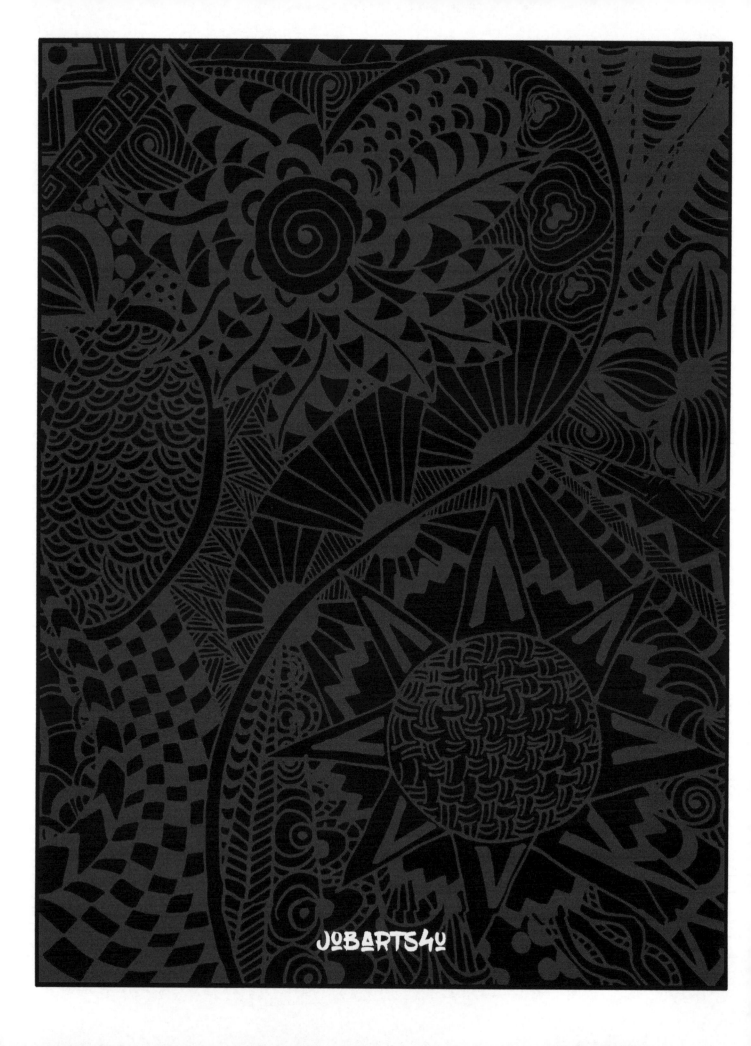

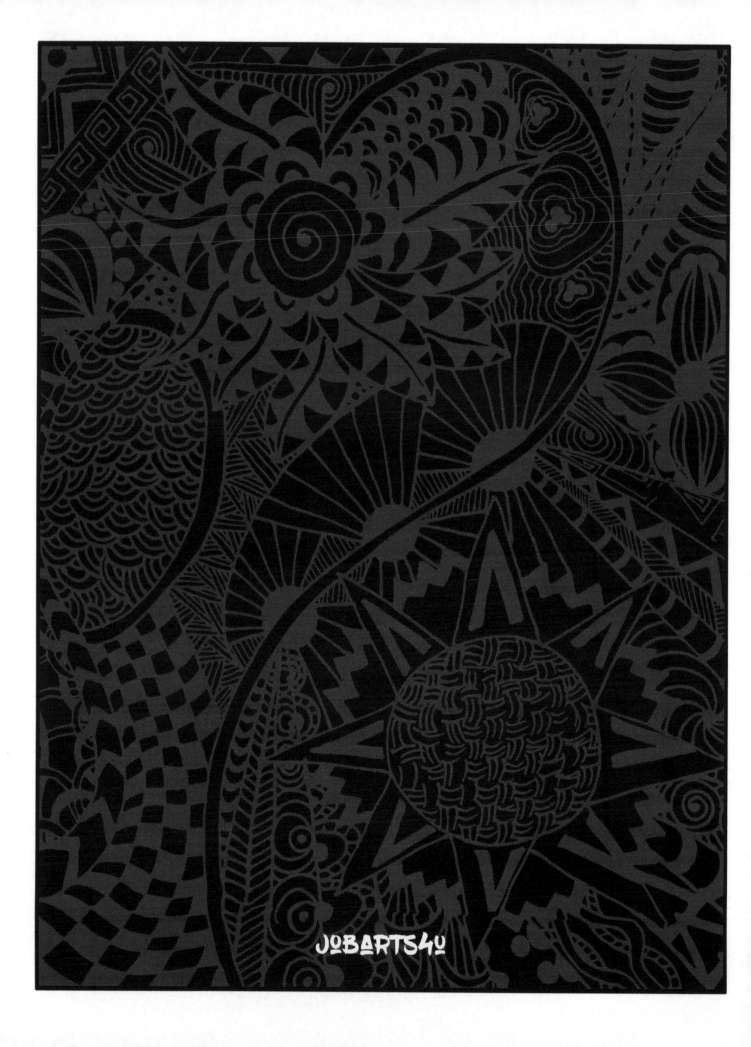

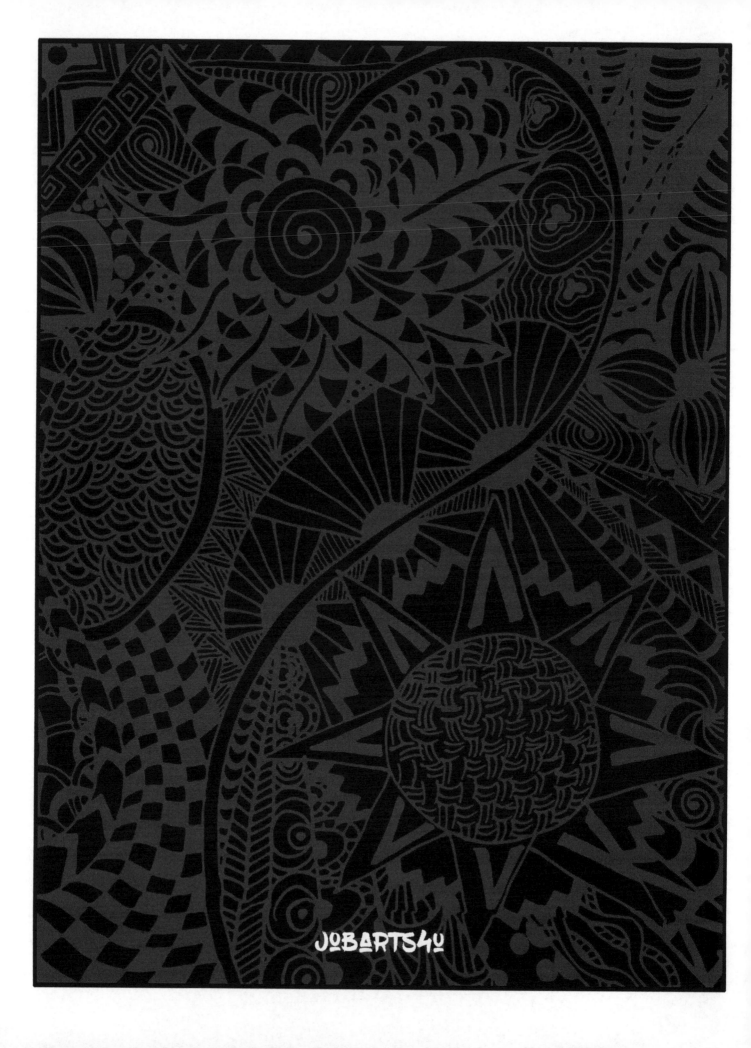

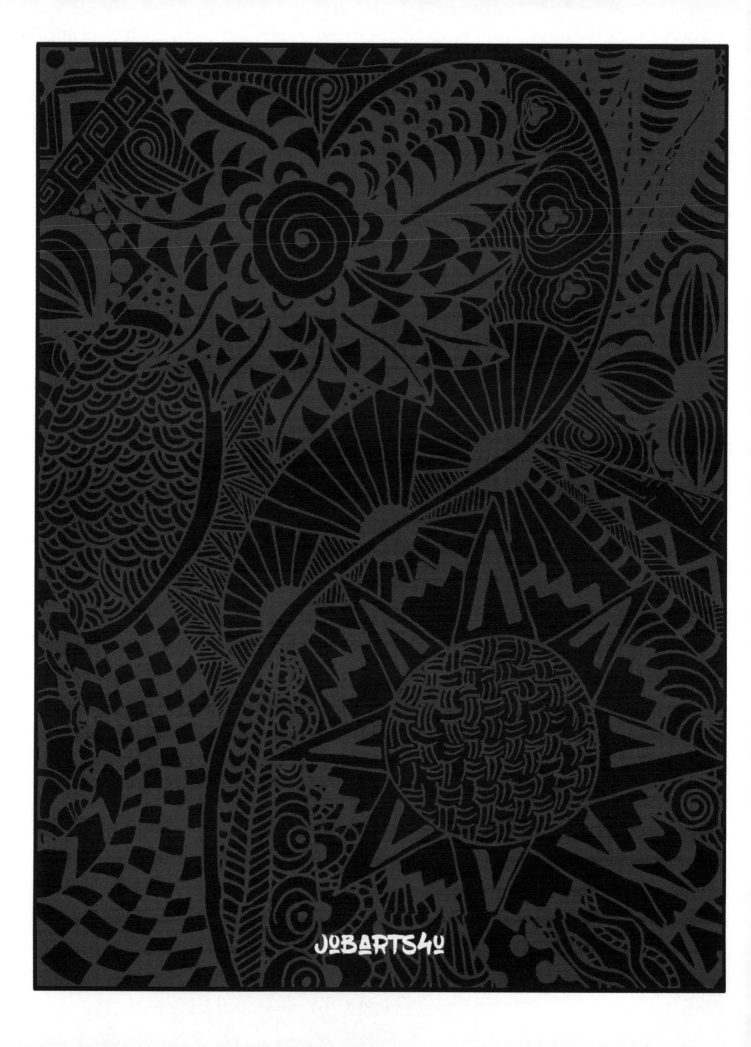

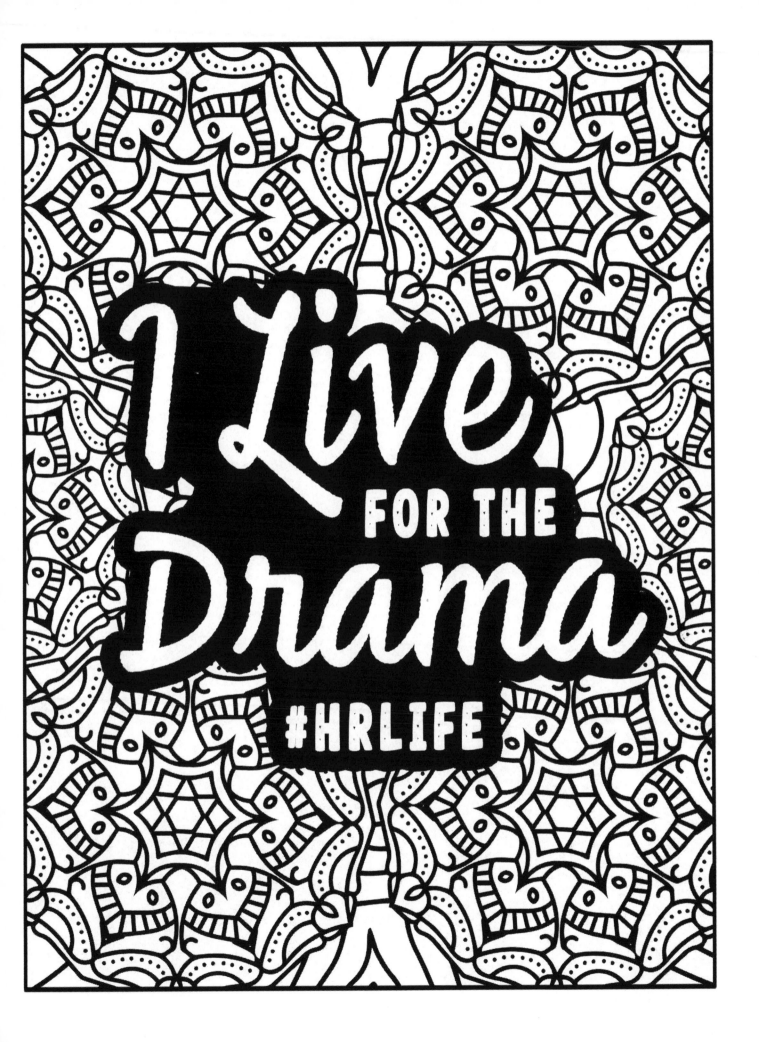

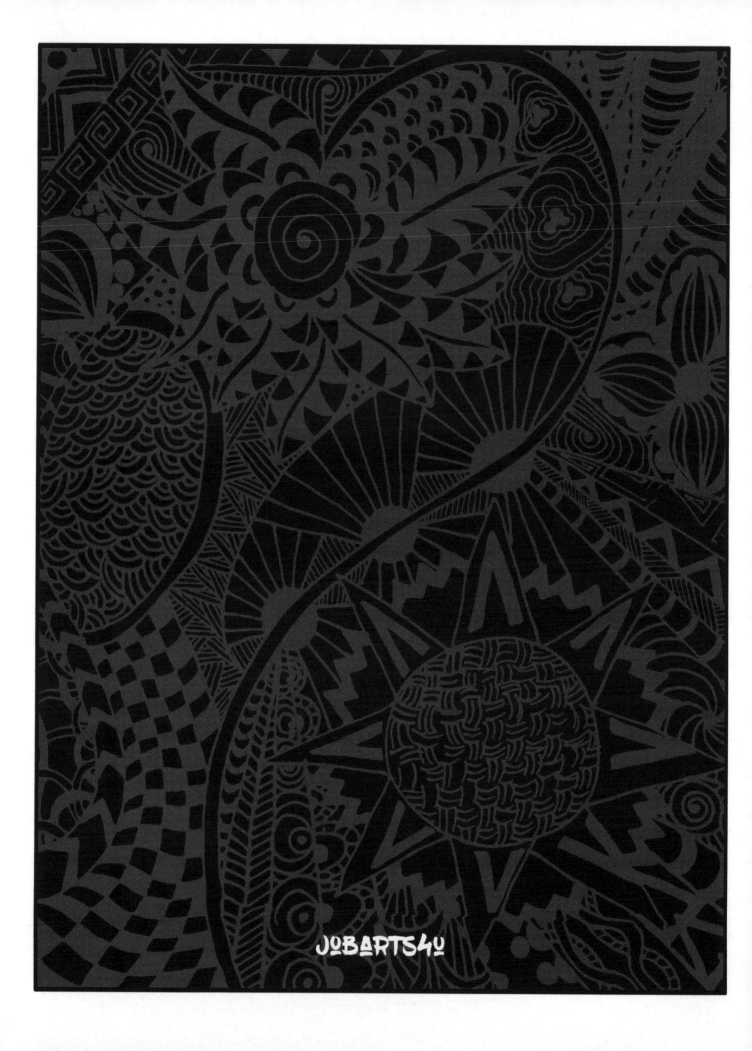

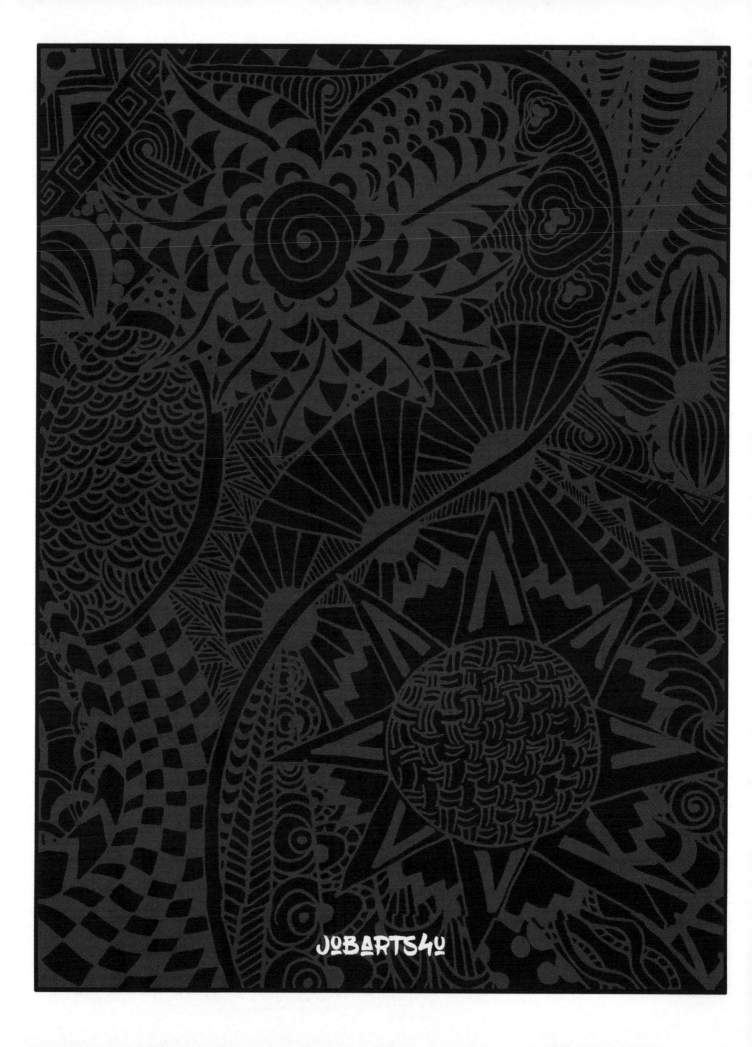

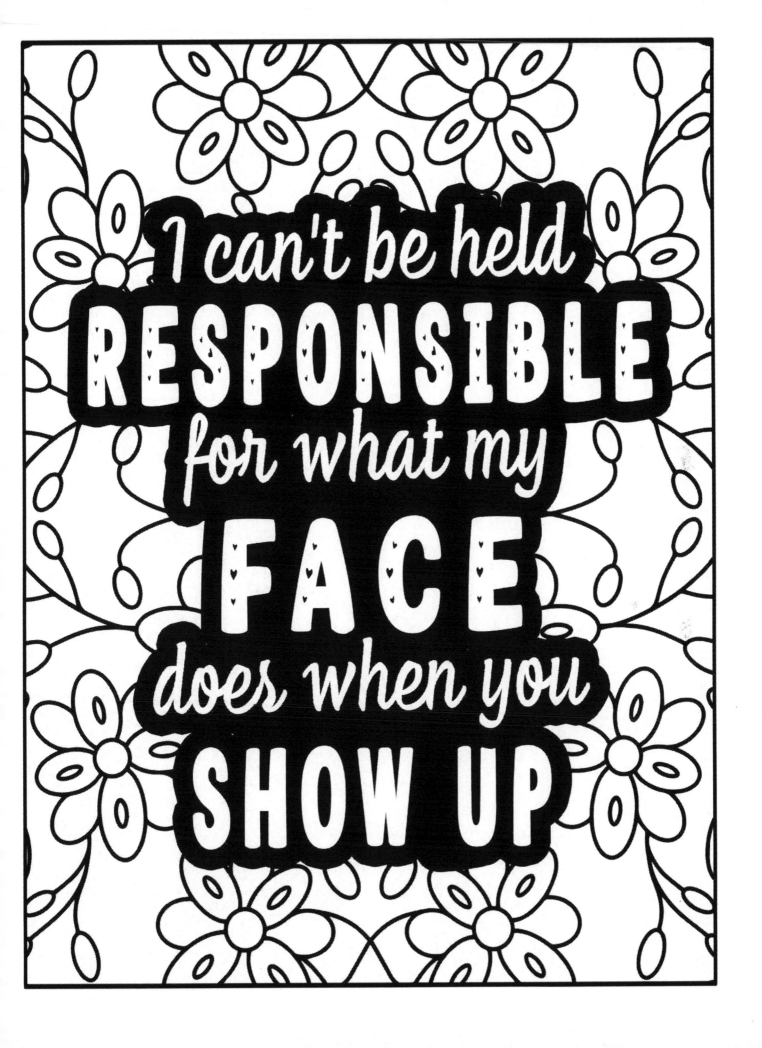

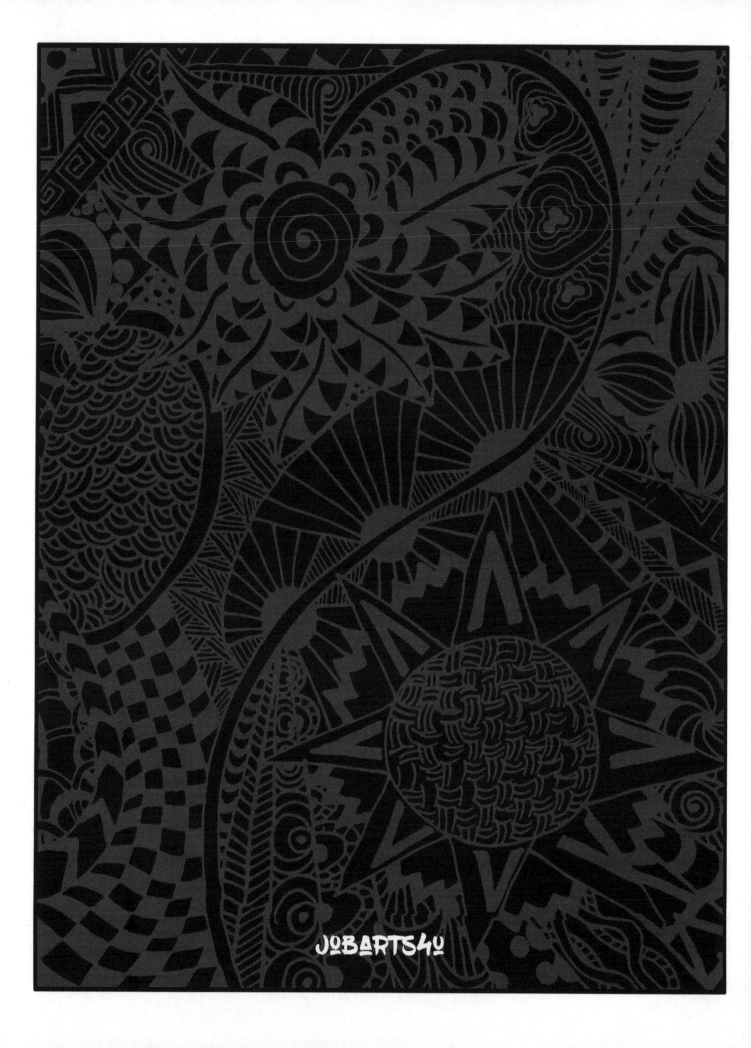

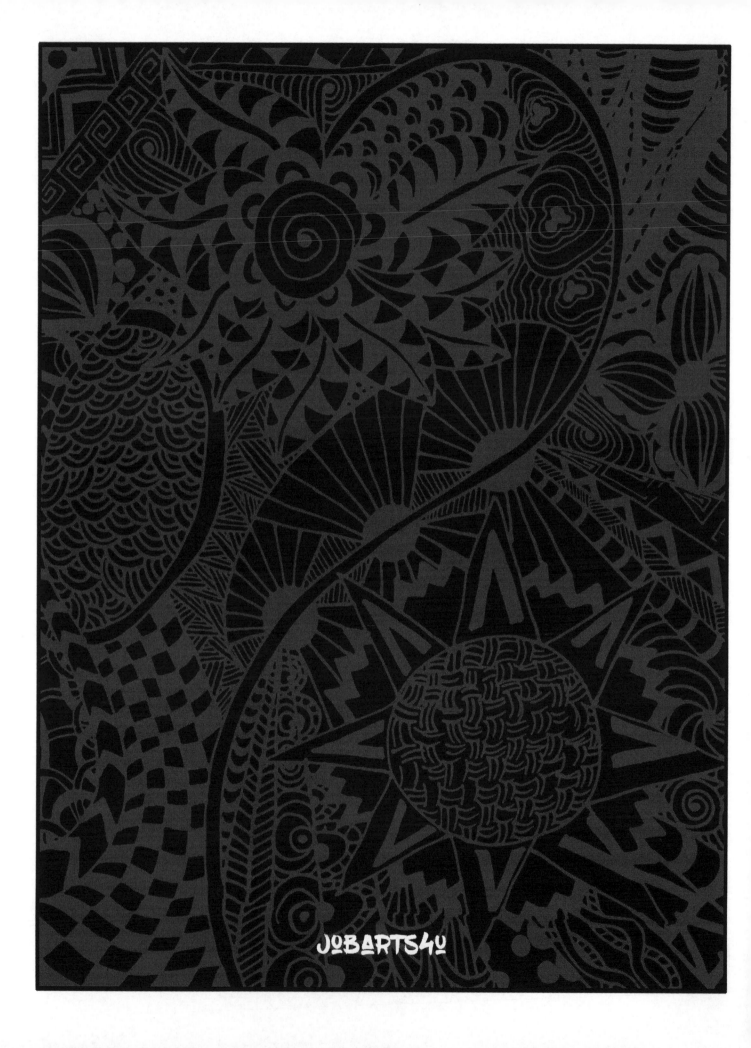

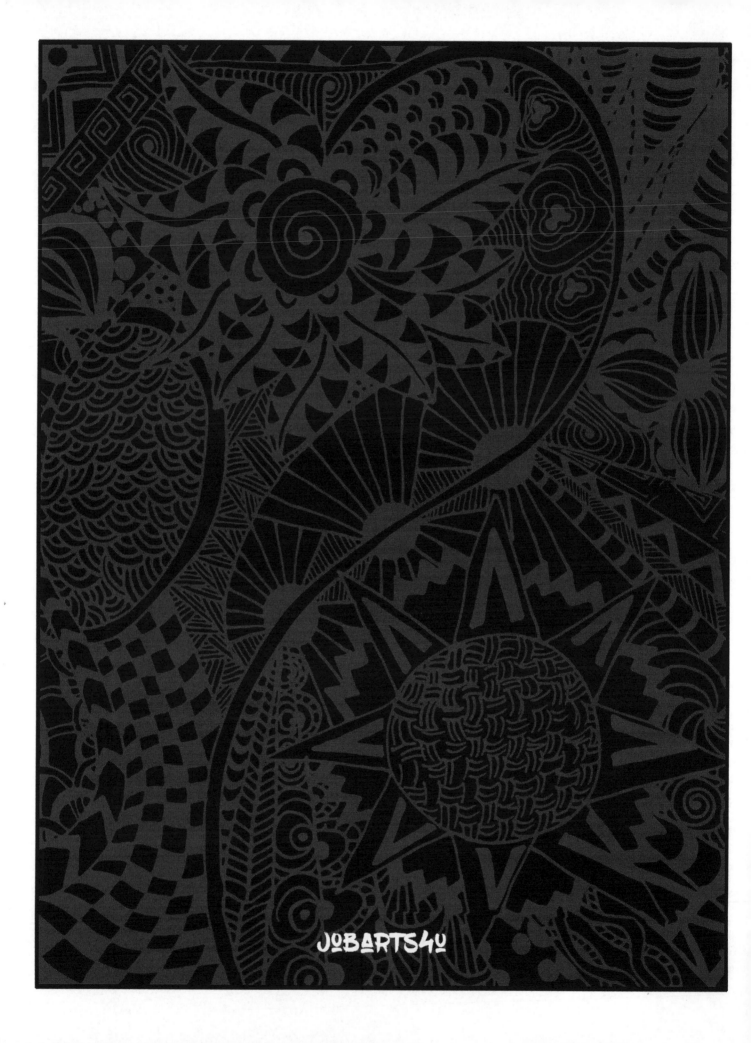

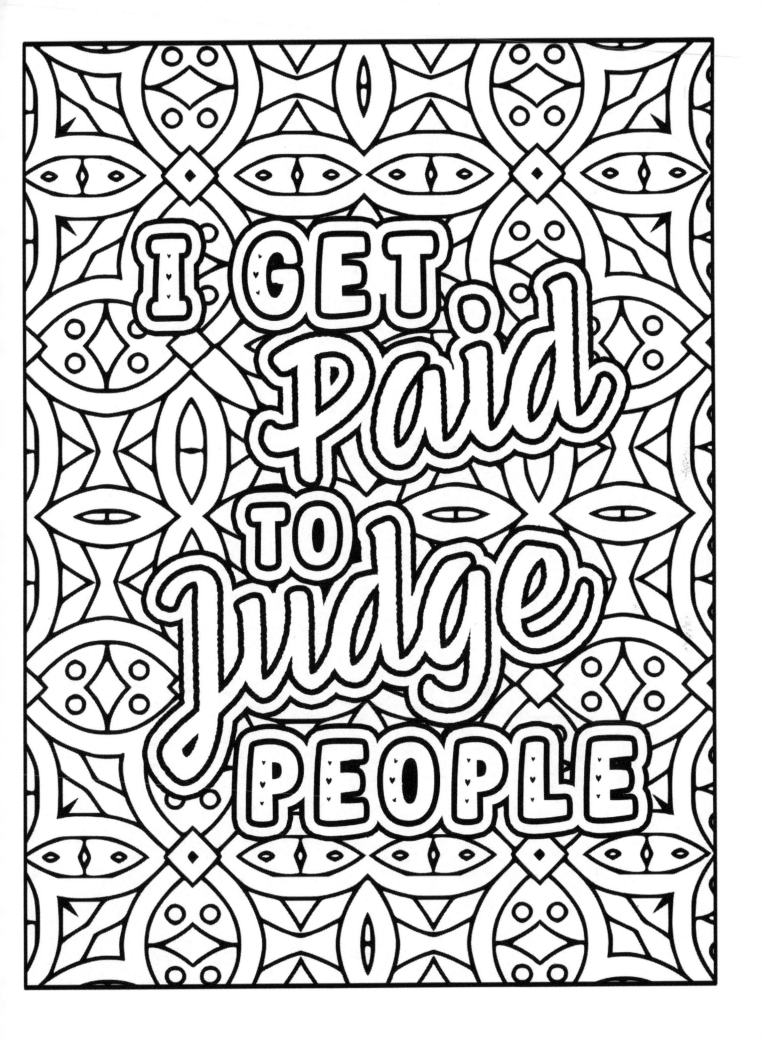

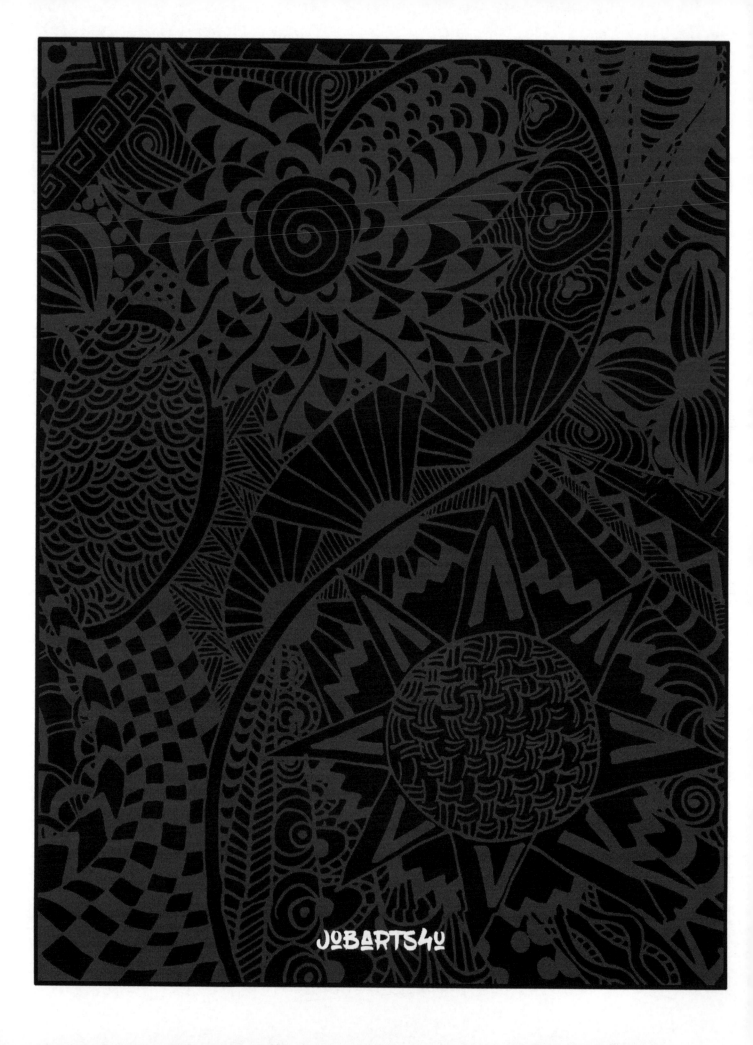

Sure, LET ME Drop EVERYTHING AND Work ON YOUR PROBLEM

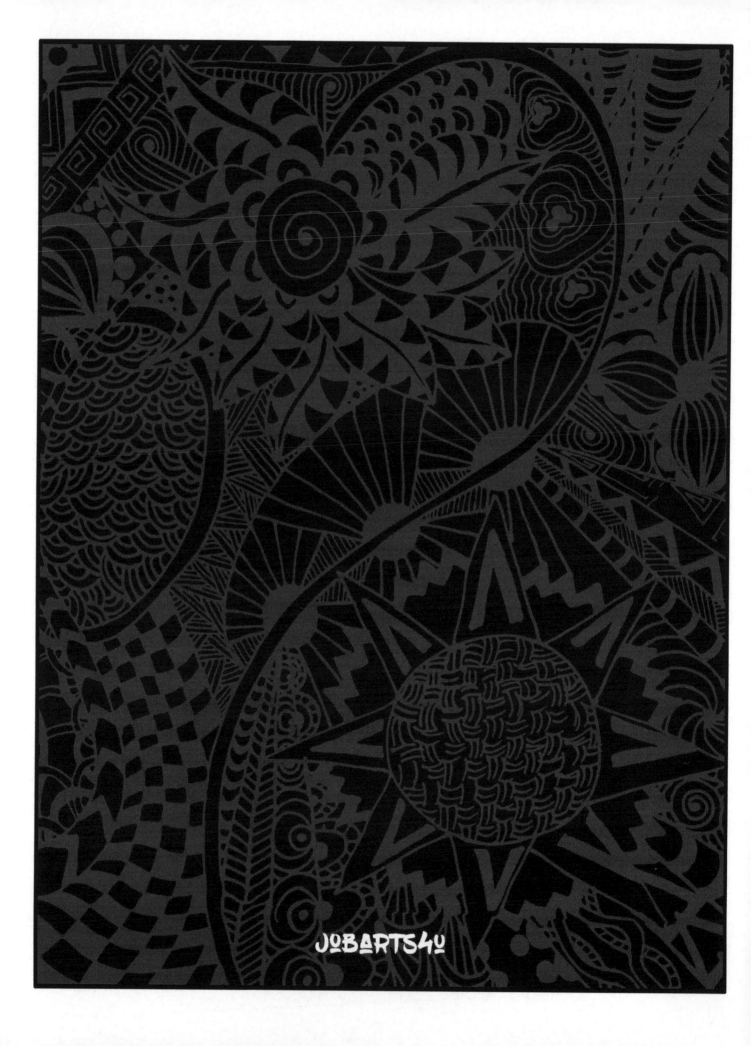

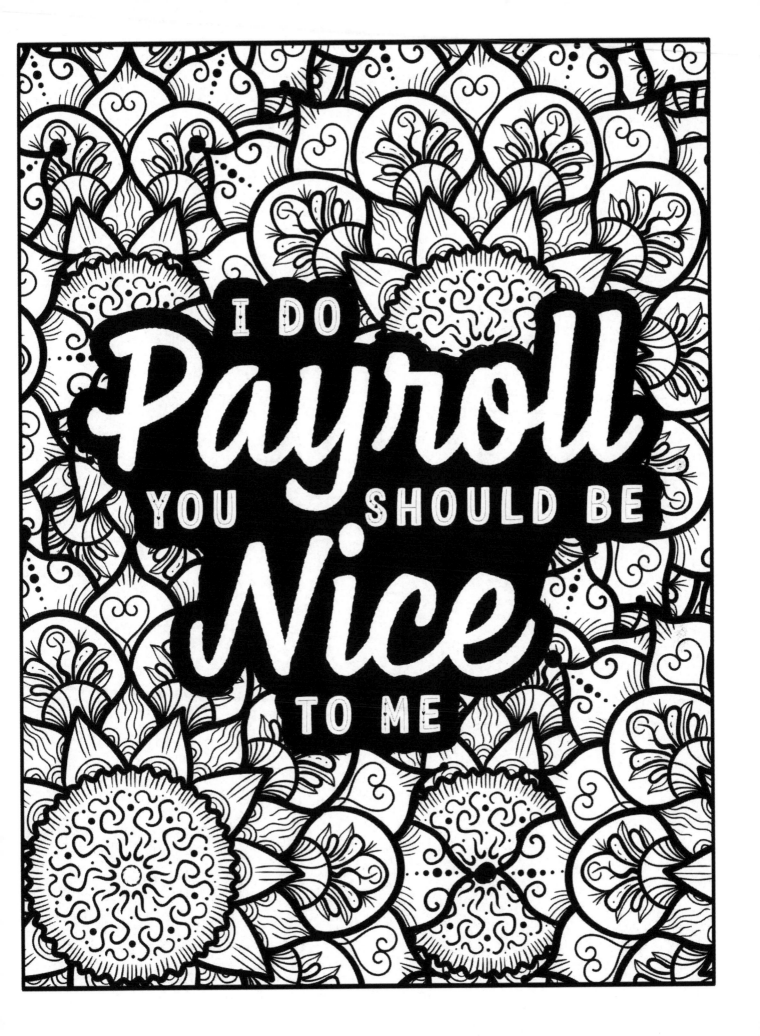

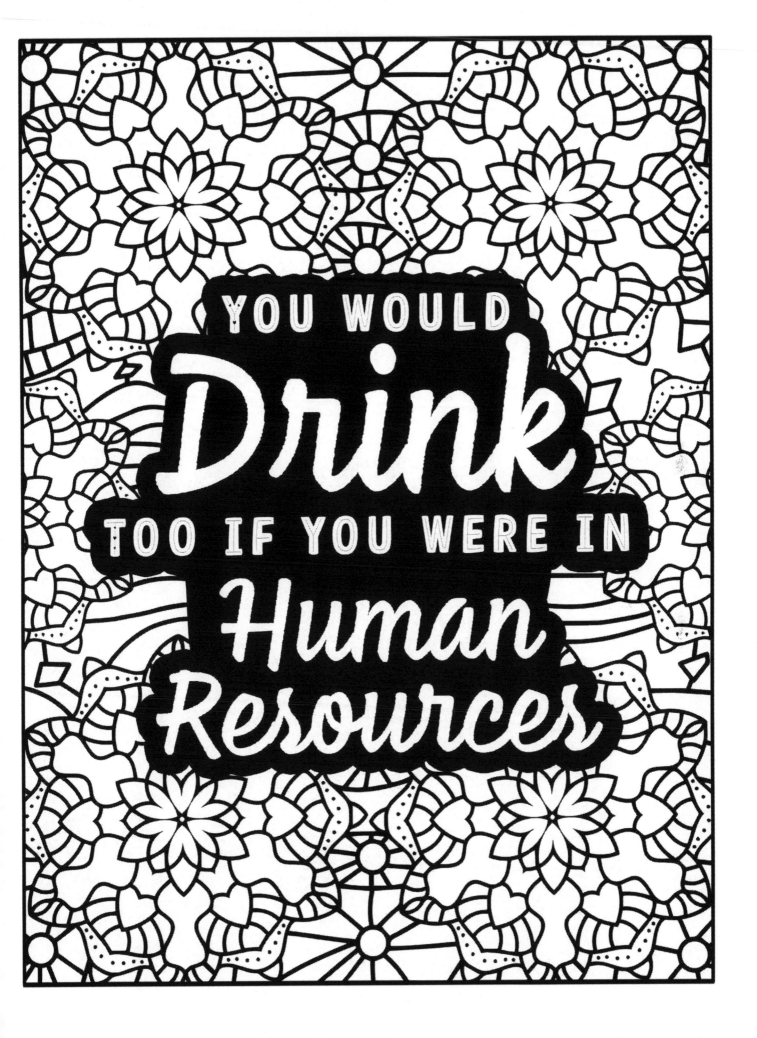

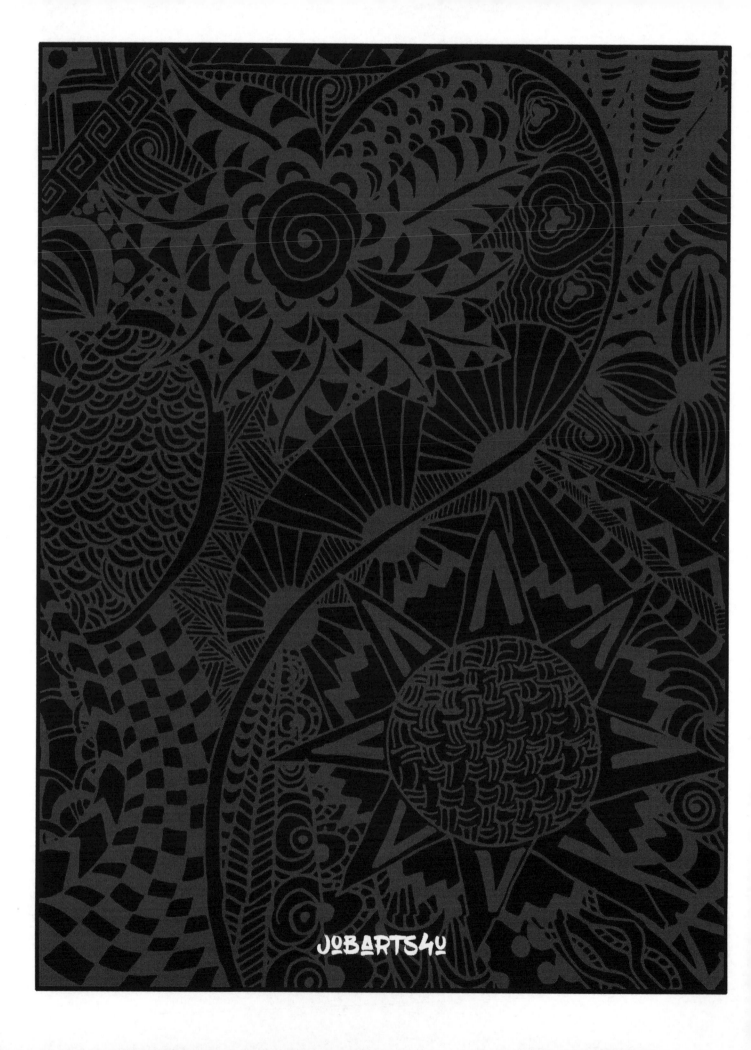

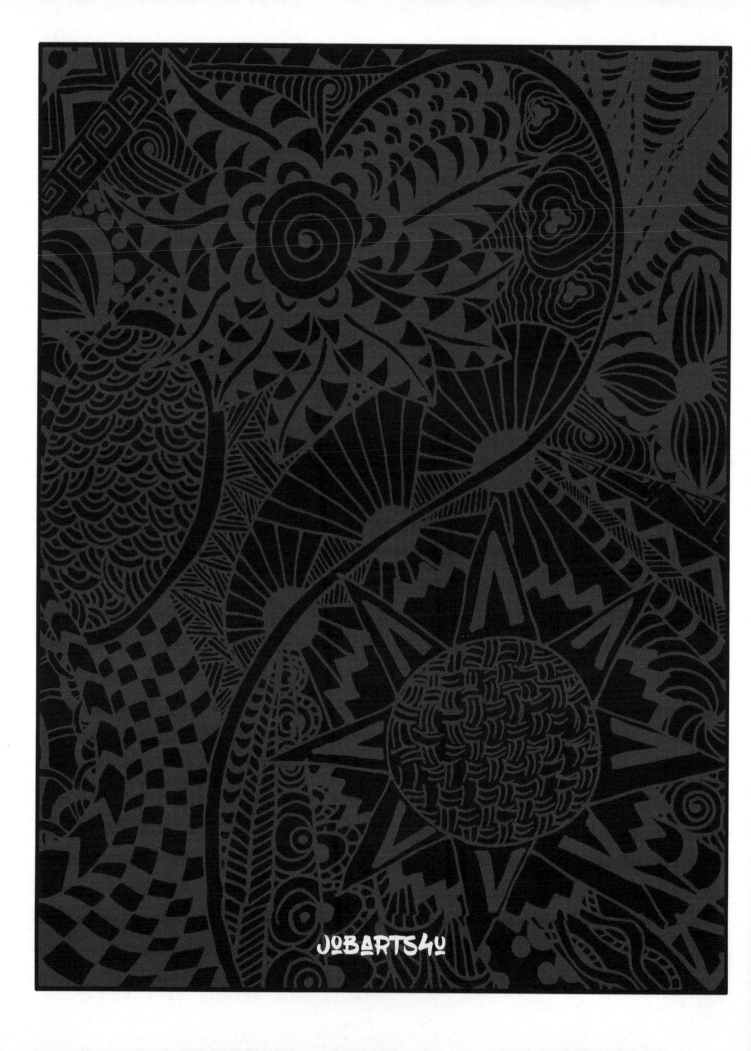

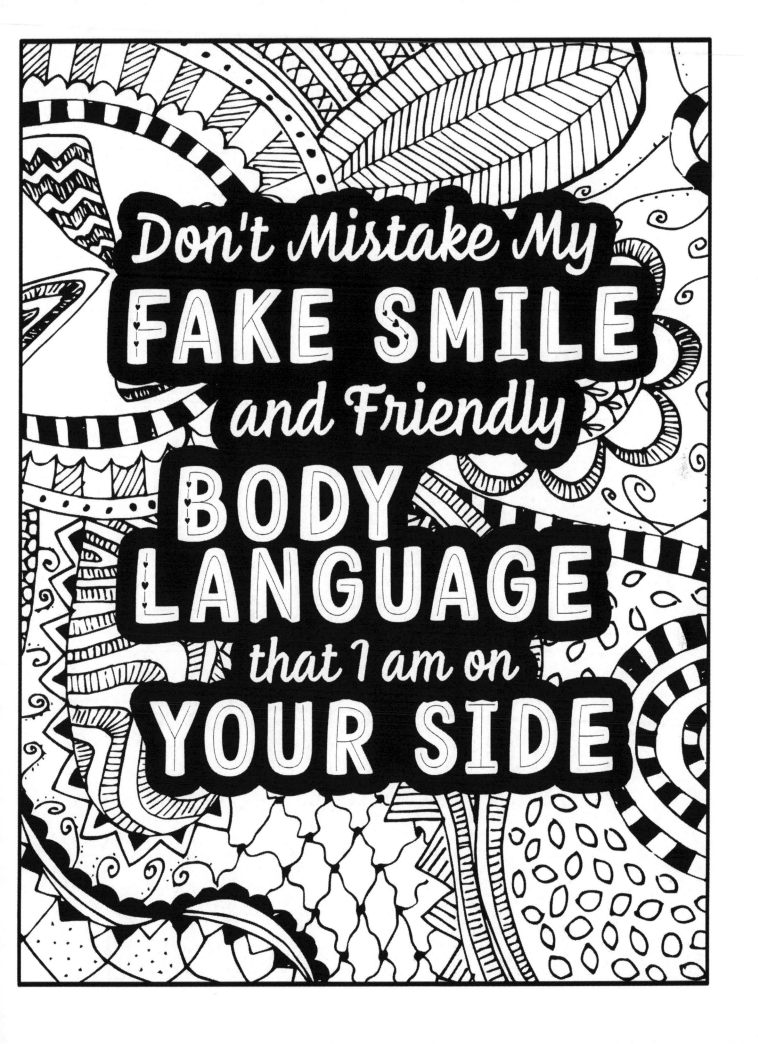

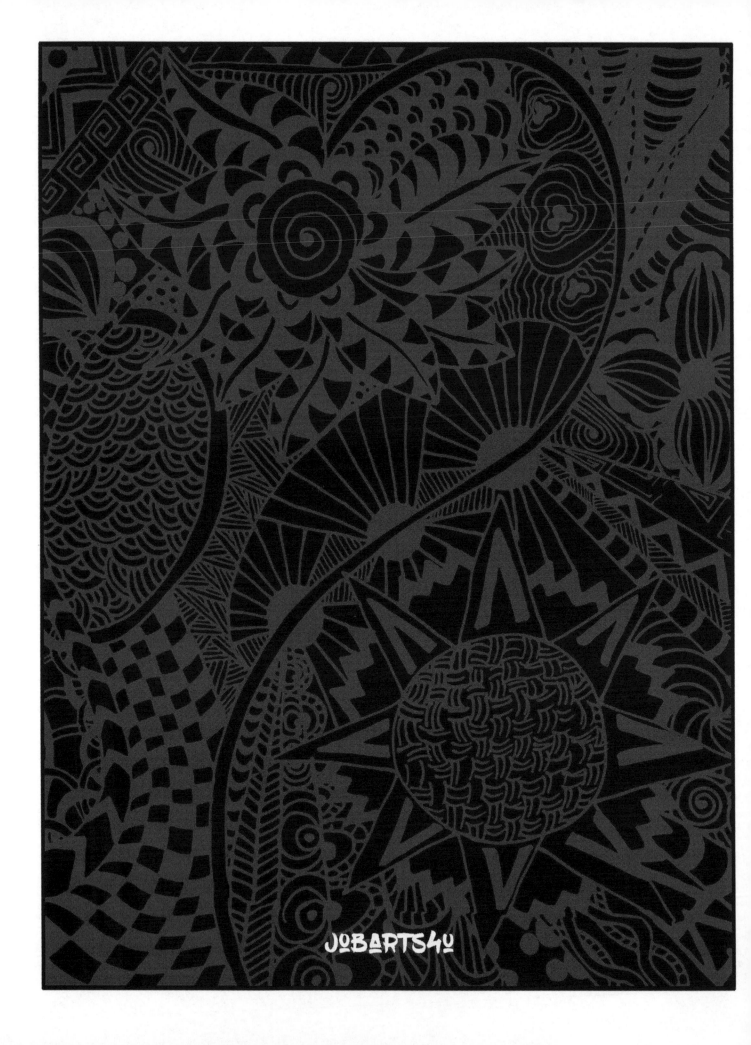

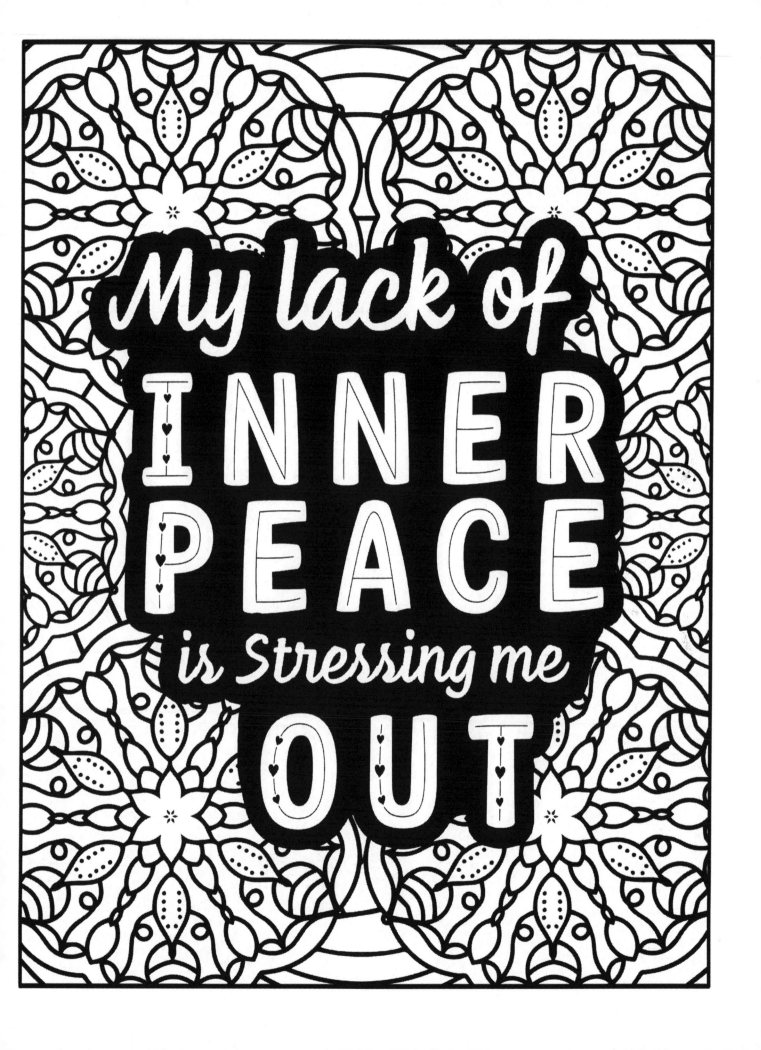

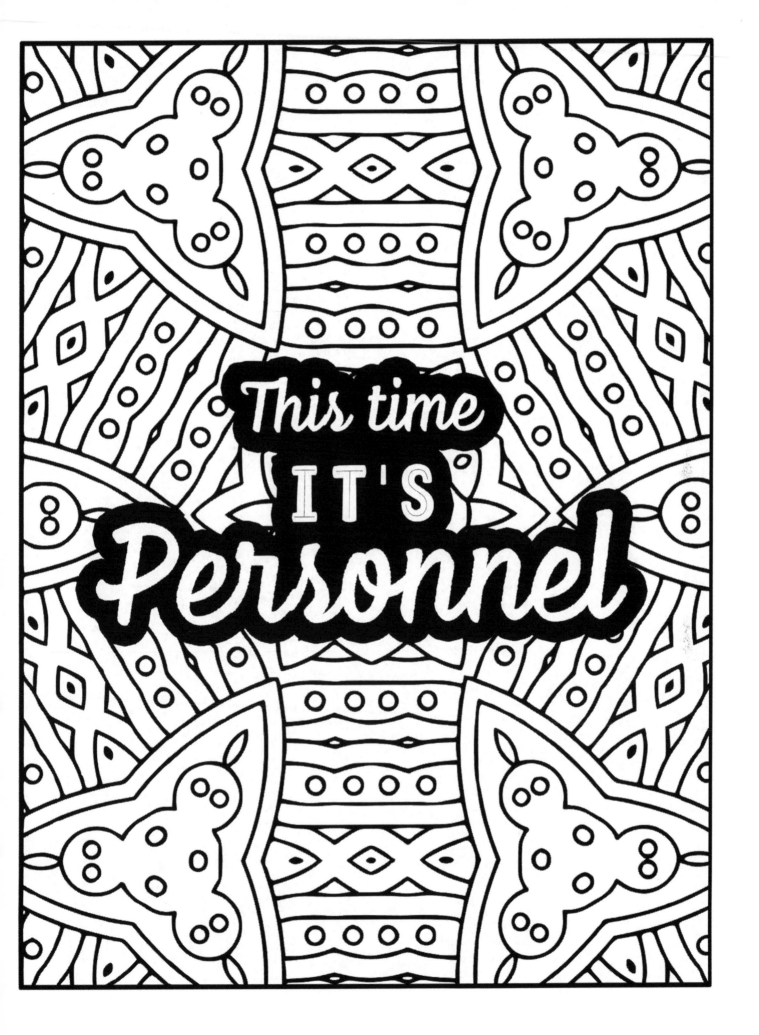

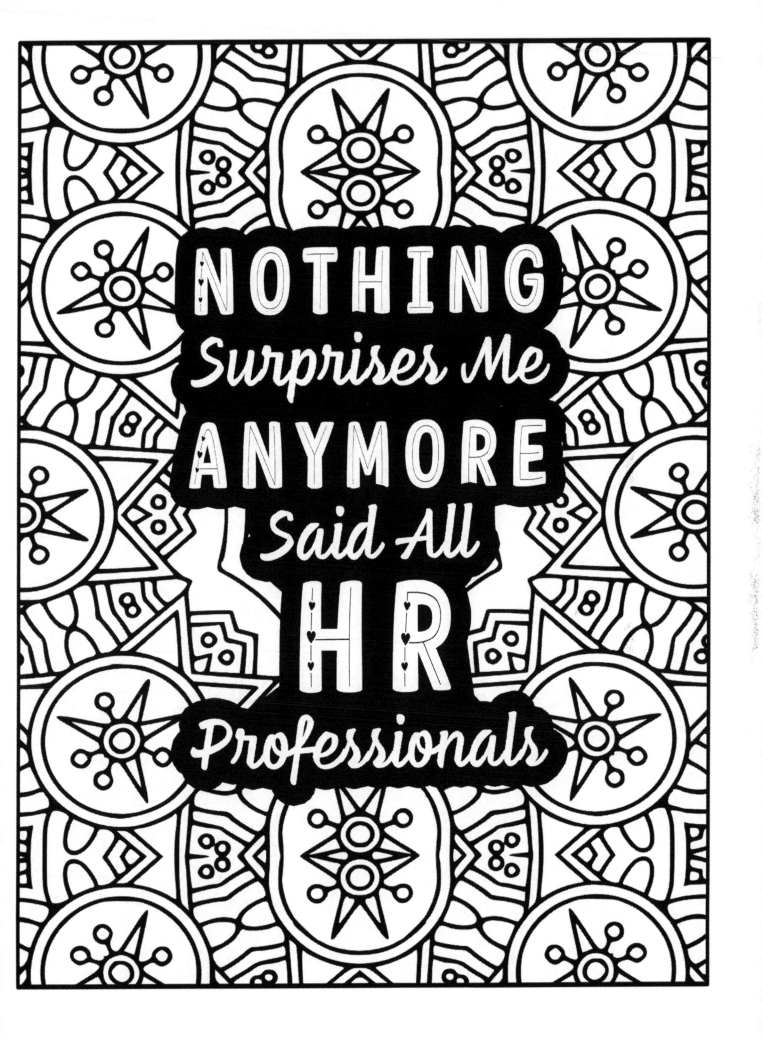

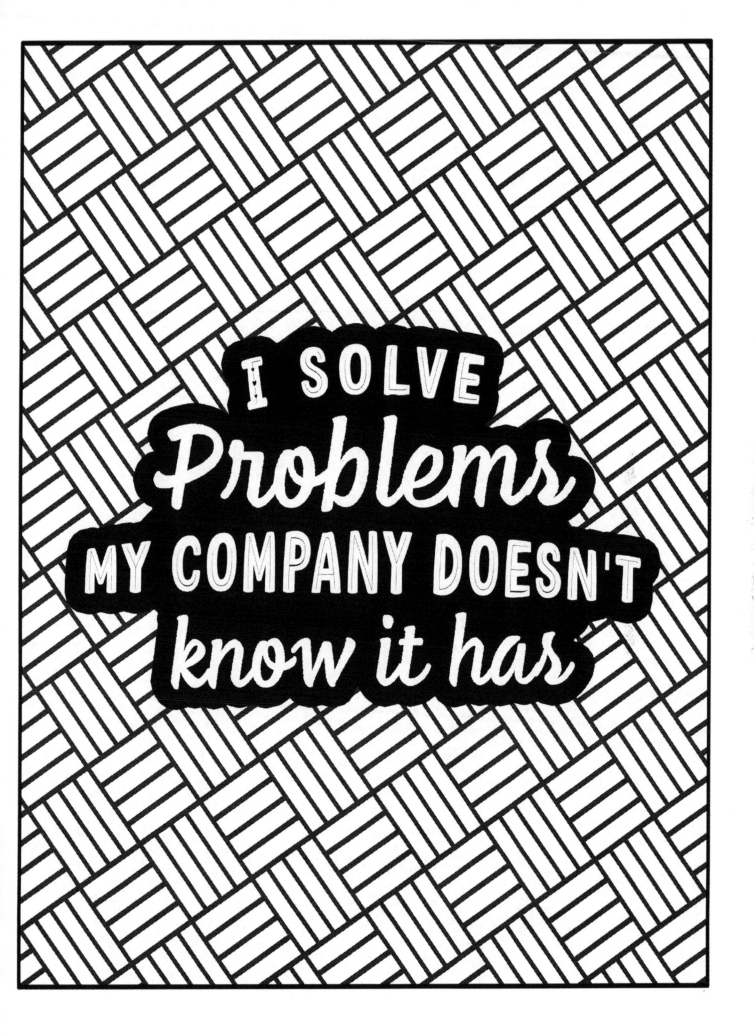

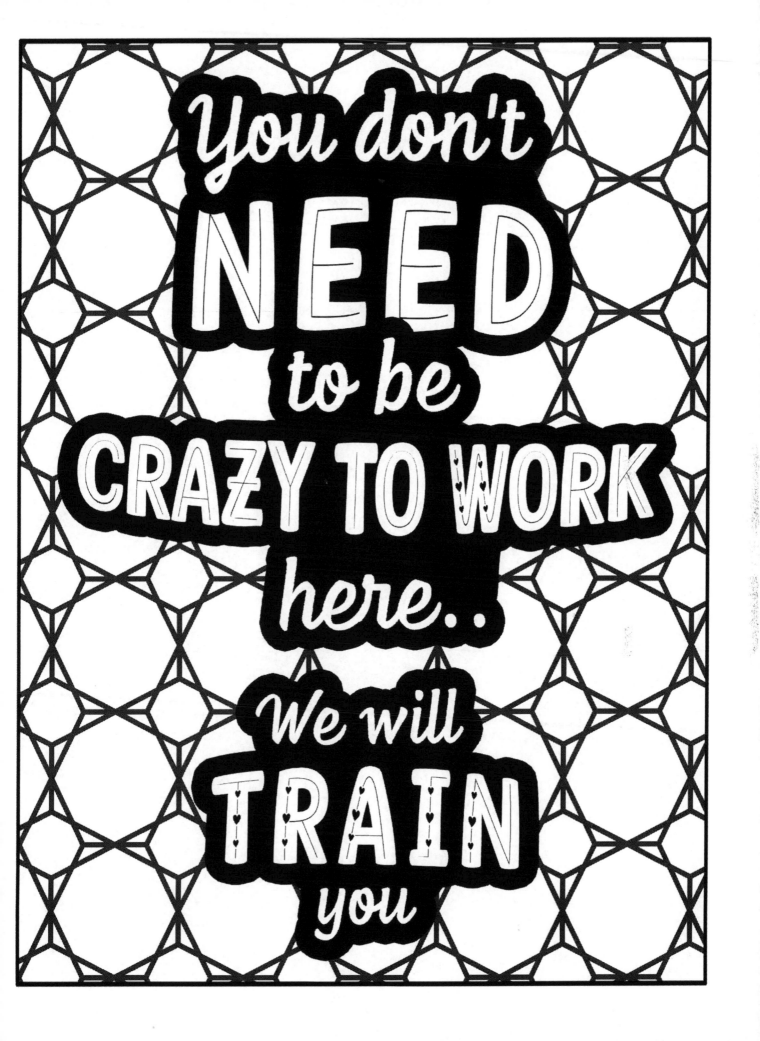

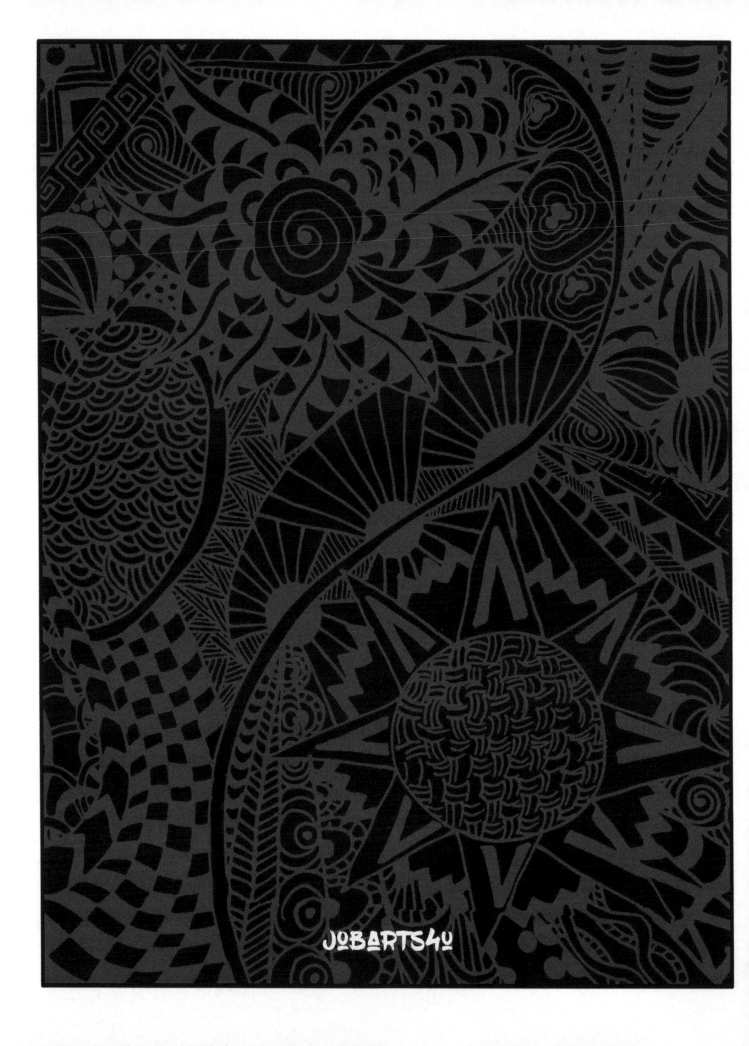

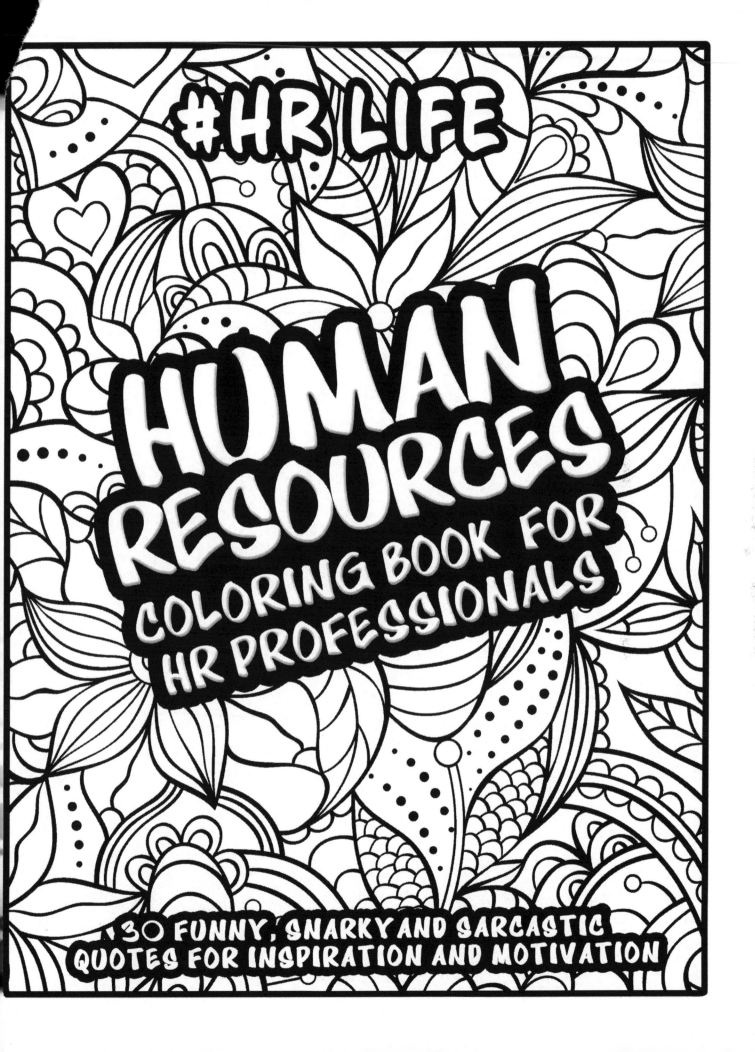

Printed in Great Britain
by Amazon

35288435R00040